## SOLO PIANO

# ESSENTIAL FILM THEMES

### THE FINEST MUSIC FROM TODAY'S OUTSTANDING FILMS

Published by
**WISE PUBLICATIONS**
14-15 Berners Street, London W1T 3LJ, UK.

Exclusive Distributors:
**MUSIC SALES LIMITED**
Distribution Centre, Newmarket Road, Bury St. Edmunds, Suffolk IP33 3YB, UK.
**MUSIC SALES PTY LIMITED**
120 Rothschild Avenue, Rosebery, NSW 2018, Australia.

Order No. AM991287
ISBN 978-1-84772-195-2
This book © Copyright 2007 Wise Publications,
a division of Music Sales Limited.

Compiled by Nick Crispin.
Edited by Ann Barkway.
Arranging and engraving supplied by Camden Music.
Arrangements by Jeremy Birchall & Christopher Hussey.
Printed in the EU.

Your Guarantee of Quality
As publishers, we strive to produce every book to the highest commercial standards.
This book has been carefully designed to minimise awkward page turns
and to make playing from it a real pleasure.
Particular care has been given to specifying acid-free, neutral-sized paper made
from pulps which have not been elemental chlorine bleached.
This pulp is from farmed sustainable forests and was produced with special regard for the environment.
Throughout, the printing and binding have been planned to ensure a sturdy,
attractive publication which should give years of enjoyment.
If your copy fails to meet our high standards, please inform us and we will gladly replace it.

www.musicsales.com

**WISE PUBLICATIONS**
part of The Music Sales Group
London/New York/Paris/Sydney/Copenhagen/Berlin/Madrid/Tokyo

# ATONEMENT

COMPOSED BY DARIO MARIANELLI

**LOVE LETTERS**

**Allegro non troppo, con molto rubato** ♩ = c.144

A tempo (con rubato)

5

molto rit.    Più lento    rall.

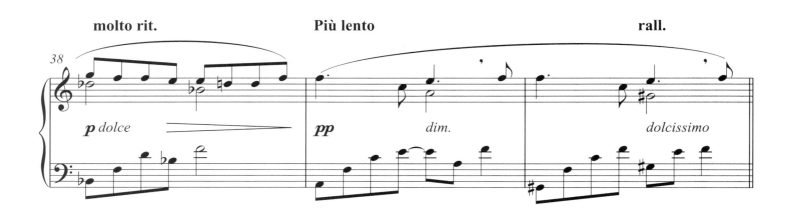

A tempo (con rubato)

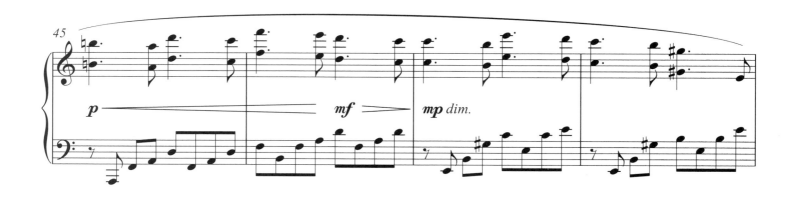

molto rit.      Più lento

molto rit.

# BECOMING JANE

### COMPOSED BY ADRIAN JOHNSTON

**FIRST IMPRESSIONS**

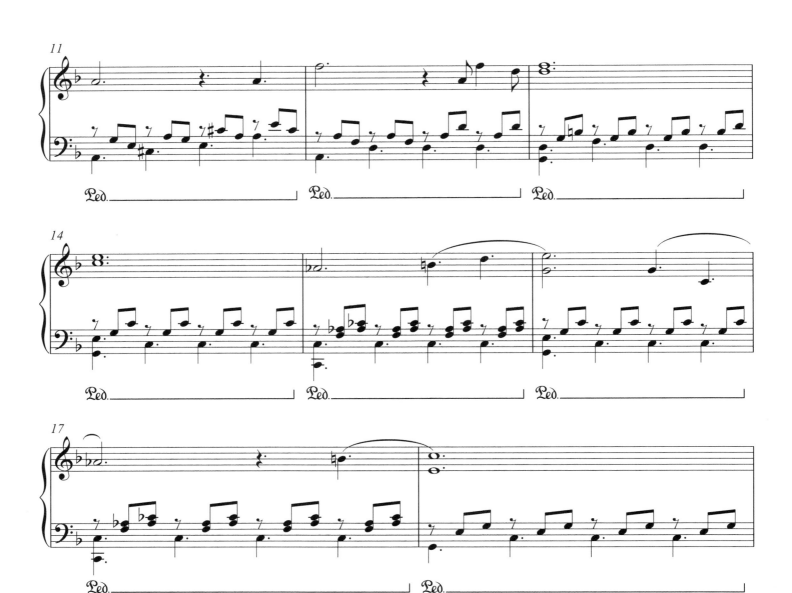

**SELBOURNE WOOD**

Andante ♩ = c.72

mp

LADY GRESHAM

rit.

Con moto ♩ = 84

11

RUNAWAYS
Moderato ♩ = 80

AN ADORING HEART

# BLADES OF GLORY

COMPOSED BY THEODORE SHAPIRO

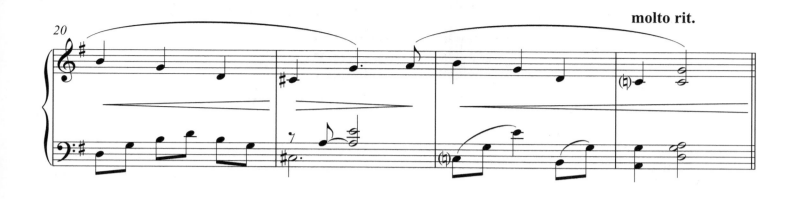

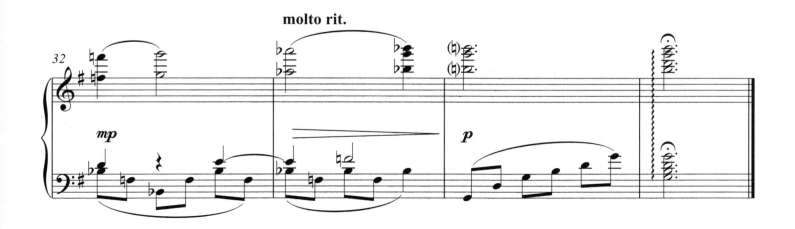

# THE BOURNE ULTIMATUM

COMPOSED BY JOHN POWELL

21

# CASINO ROYALE

COMPOSED BY DAVID ARNOLD

**VESPER**

Slowly ♩ = 60

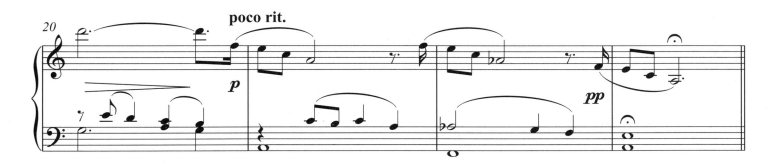

## THE CITY OF LOVERS

**Più mosso** ♩ = 70

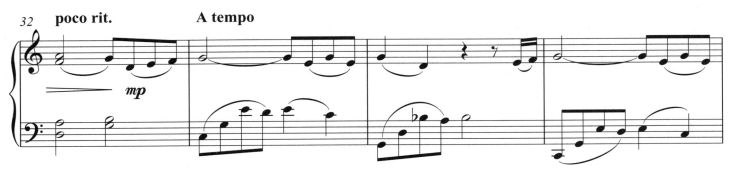

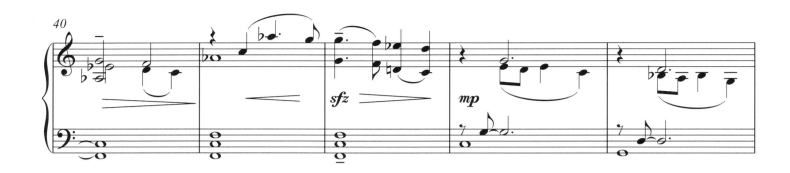

### THE NAME'S BOND... JAMES BOND

**Menacingly** ♩ = 80

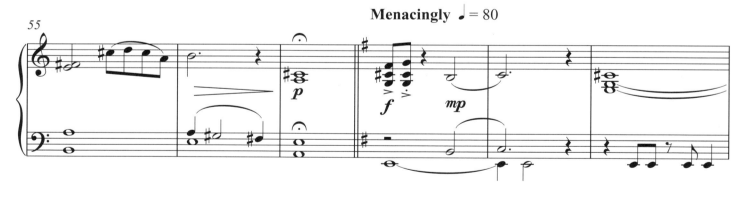

con moto

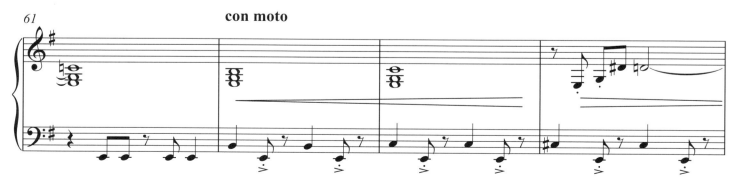

27

# DEATH PROOF

COMPOSED BY PINO DONAGGIO

**SALLY AND JACK**

**Teneramente, con rubato** ♩ = c.60

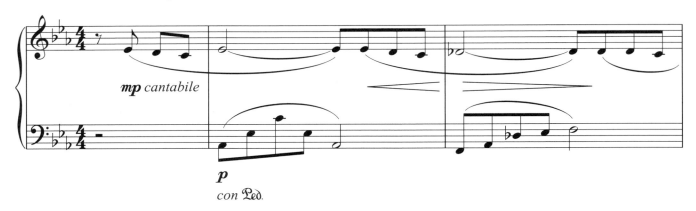

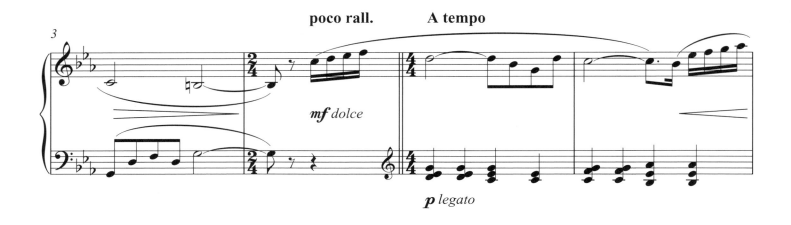

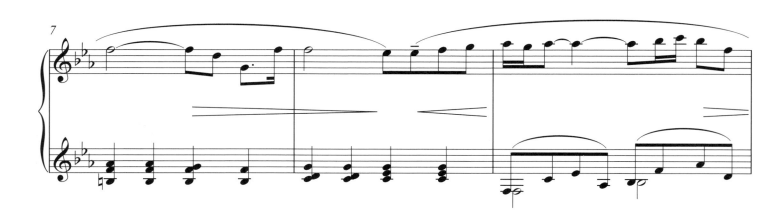

poco rall.

**A tempo**

**Più mosso**

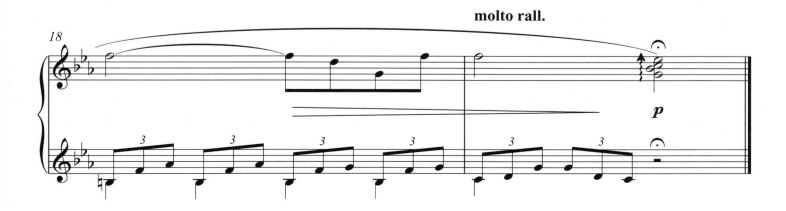

molto rall.

# DIE HARD 4.0

## COMPOSED BY MARCO BELTRAMI

**LIVE FREE OR DIE HARD**

**Energetically and with menace** ♩ = 142

# FANTASTIC FOUR: RISE OF THE SILVER SURFER

## COMPOSED BY JOHN OTTMAN

**SILVER SURFER THEME**

Calmly ♩ = 80

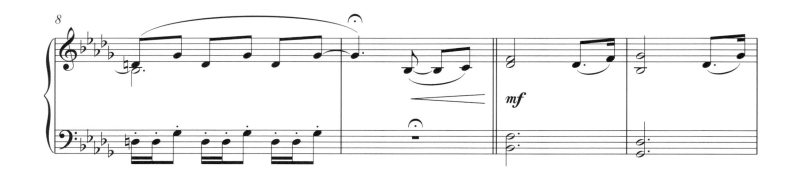

39

# IL CAIMANO/LE CAÏMAN

COMPOSED BY FRANCO PIERSANTI

**PAOLO E BRUNO**

*molto rubato*

Ped. _____

molto rit.　　　　A tempo

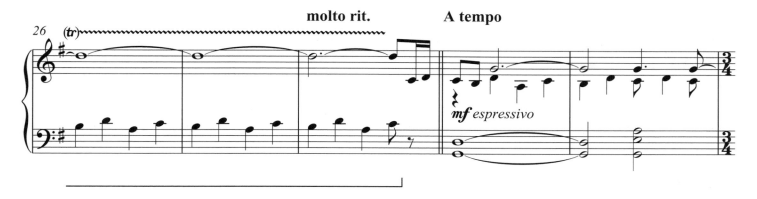

*mf espressivo*

poco rit.

A tempo

# THE GOOD SHEPHERD

COMPOSED BY MARCELO ZARVOS

48

**EDWARD'S SECRET**

**Lento con rubato**  ♩ = 60

# JINDABYNE

COMPOSED BY PAUL KELLY & DAN LUSCOMBE

**STEWART AND CLAIRE**
Più mosso ♩ = 112

*p cantabile*

to Coda ⊕

con Ped.

THE HUMMING WAY

**Meno mosso, swung** ♩ = 90

57

rit. poco a poco

# LETTERS FROM IWO JIMA

## COMPOSED BY KYLE EASTWOOD & MICHAEL STEVENS

sempre Ped.

61

# LITTLE CHILDREN

COMPOSED BY THOMAS NEWMAN

**2 HILLCREST**

**Like a subdued nursery rhyme** ♩. = 50

**POOL DAYS**

**Slightly faster, like a slow waltz** ♩ = 80

**END TITLES**

Elegantly ♩. = 50

**Very hazily and dreamy, with rubato** ♩ = 50

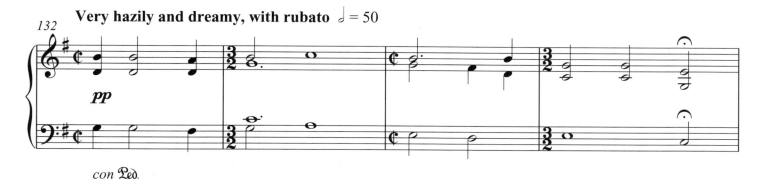

*pp*

*con Ped.*

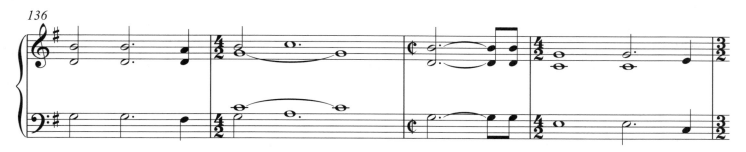

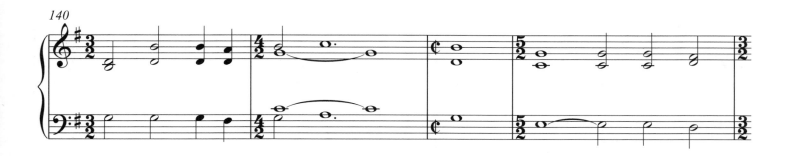

*ppp*

# THE LIVES OF OTHERS

COMPOSED BY GABRIEL YARED & STÉPHANE MOUCHA

**DAS LEBEN DER ANDEREN**

Largo ♩ = 54

IM "MARTHA"

**Con moto** ♩ = 132

73

GESICHTER DER LIEBE

Meno mosso ♩ = 66

# THE PAINTED VEIL

COMPOSED BY ALEXANDRE DESPLAT

**THE PAINTED VEIL**

**Allegro marcato** ♩ = 126

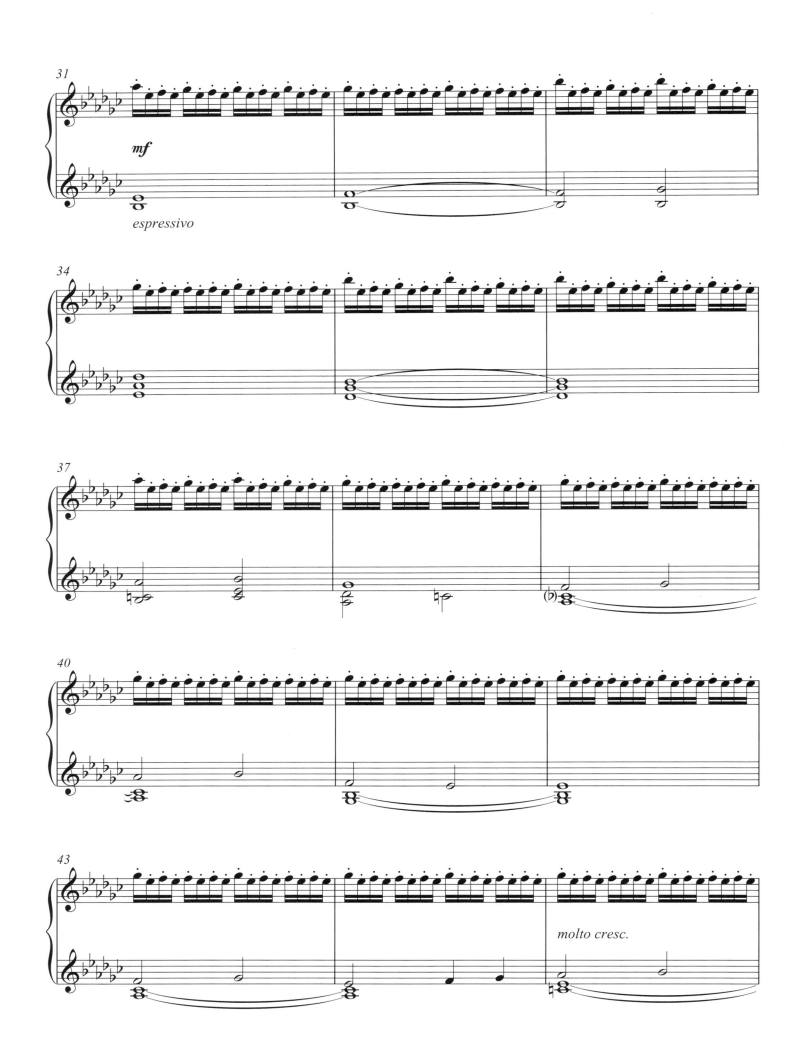

## RIVER WALTZ

**Moderato, con rubato** ♩ = 112

PROMENADE

**Con moto** ♩ = 58

loco

*mf*

*mp espressivo*

*pp*

Ped.

Ped.

# LONDON TO BRIGHTON

## COMPOSED BY LAURA ROSSI

**END CREDITS**

**Più mosso** ♩= 120

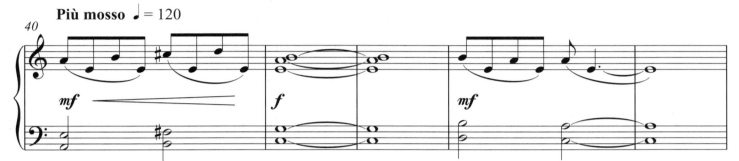

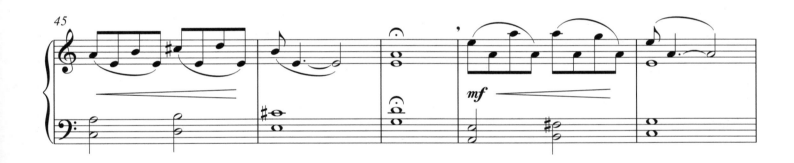

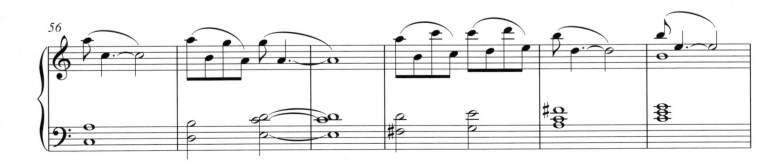

# RUN FAT BOY RUN

COMPOSED BY ALEX WURMAN

**GOING ON HOLIDAY**

**Heroically** ♩ = 114

# THE SIMPSONS MOVIE

## COMPOSED BY HANS ZIMMER

**DOOMSDAY IS FAMILY TIME**

**Joyfully** ♩ = 120

# THIS IS ENGLAND

COMPOSED BY LUDOVICO EINAUDI

103

# ZODIAC

COMPOSED BY DAVID SHIRE

**GRAYSMITH'S THEME**

Rubato ♩ = c.58

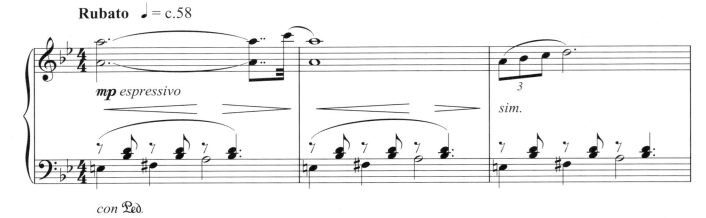

con Ped.

poco rit.          A tempo                          poco rit.

A tempo

rit.          A tempo

poco rit.

A tempo, più mosso

poco rit.          A tempo

TOSCHI'S THEME

# STRANGER THAN FICTION

## COMPOSED BY BRIAN REITZELL & BRITT DANIEL

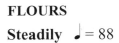

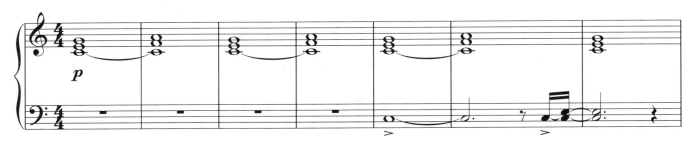

# WRITER'S BLOCK

Freely ♩ = c.52

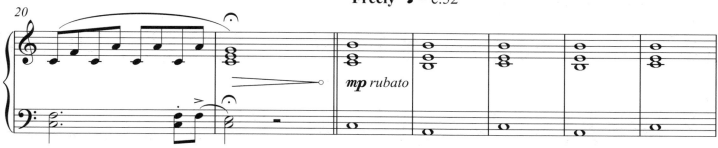

con Ped.

Più mosso ♩ = c.60

Ped._____

poco rit.    Tempo I ♩ = c.54

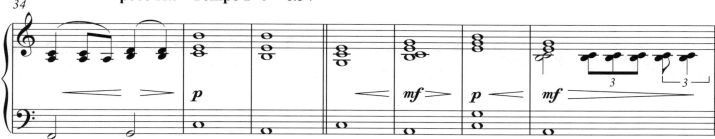

Più mosso ♩ = c.60

rit.

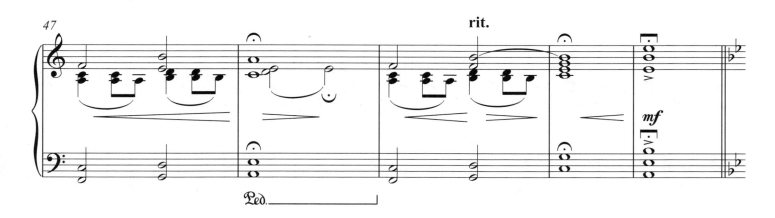

Ped._____

109

**AUDITOR**

**With a steady beat** ♩ = 124

**Smoothly and broadly**

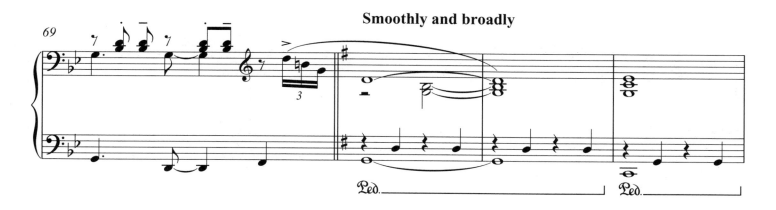

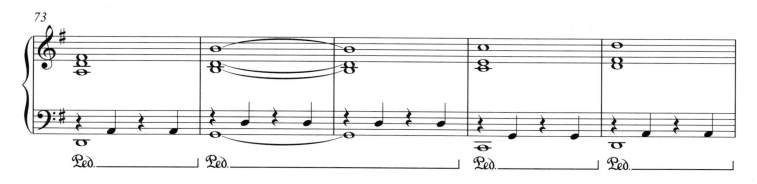

**A tempo, with a steady beat**

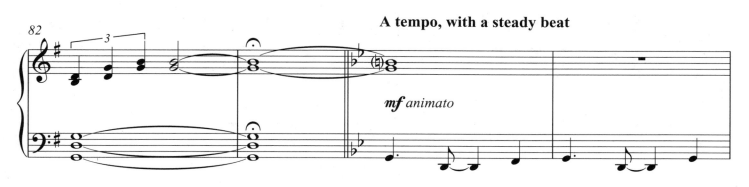

7/08 (166390)   2 3 4 5 6 7 8 9